Cathedral Music Press Presents

Sacred Melodies for Violin Solo

KEYBOARD ACCOMPANIMENT INCLUDED

Works by: Bach, Schubert, Mendelssohn, Handel, and Cesar Frank

By Craig Duncan

Cathedral
MUSIC PRESS

CONTENTS

Ave Maria

Piano

J. S. Bach - Charles Gounod

Andante con moto

Ave Maria

Piano

Franz Schubert

Air for the G String

from the Orchestral Suite Number 3 in D

Piano

J. S. Bach

Lento

But the Lord is Mindful of His Own

Aria from St. Paul

Piano

Felix Mendelssohn

13

He Shall Feed His Flock

from The Messiah

Piano

G. F. Handel

Kanon

Piano

Johann Pachelbel

Jesu, Joy of Man's Desiring

Chorale from Cantata Number 147

Piano

J. S. Bach

Moderato

O Holy Night

Piano

Adolphe Adam

Panis Angelicus

O, Lord Most Holy

Piano

Cesar Franck

Poco Lento

rallentando

rallentando

p a tempo

p a tempo

pp

The Palms

Piano

Jean-Baptiste Faure

Andante Maestoso

Songs Without Words

Felix Mendelssohn Op. 19, No. 1

Piano

Andante con moto

Sheep May Safely Graze

from the Birthday Cantata

Piano

J. S. Bach

Andante pastorale